Tasha Tudor's
OLD-FASHIONED GIFTS

Presents and Favors for All Occasions

Tasha Tudor and Linda Allen

DAVID McKAY COMPANY, INC.
New York

Illustrations by Tasha Tudor on pages iii, vi, 69, 97, 101, 105, 113, and 117, Courtesy of American Artists, Inc.

Library of Congress Cataloging in Publication Data

Tudor, Tasha.
Tasha Tudor's Old-fashioned gifts.

SUMMARY: Instructions for making a variety of gifts
for different holidays throughout the year.
1. Handicraft. 2. Cookery. 3. Gifts.
[1. Handicraft. 2. Cookery. 3. Gifts.]   I. Allen, Linda,
joint author.   II. Title.   III. Title: Old-fashioned gifts.
TT157.T83   745.5   79-2053
ISBN 0-679-20981-6

1 2 3 4 5 6 7 8 9 10

Manufactured in the United States of America

Book design by Jane Preston

"The only gift is a portion of thyself. Thou must bleed for me. Therefore the poet brings his poem; the shepherd, his lamb; the farmer, corn; the miner, a gem; the sailor, coral and shells; the painter, his picture; the girl, a handkerchief of her own sewing."

—Ralph Waldo Emerson
Gifts
Second series of Essays

CONTENTS

Foreword

As holidays and other celebrations approach, there is always the question: what shall I give? Of course, countless numbers of things can be bought in stores, but, somehow, store-bought presents do not always convey the warmth we hope will accompany the gifts. When people take the time and care to make the presents they give, they put into the gifts not only the materials needed, but also a part of themselves. The thoughts and feelings behind the giving, not the grandness of the gift, are the important ingredients.

We believe that the special feeling of holidays and celebrations should not be confined to just the actual day. The preparations—the secretive making of gifts, surprises, decorations, and delicacies—give those pre-celebration days an excitement of their own.

At Christmastime, for instance, the making of cornucopias, and all the delights to fill them, can be wonderful pre-holiday entertainment for children and adults alike. Pulling taffy, shaping popcorn balls, wrapping candy in cellophane and bright ribbons, making snappers with original verses, creating fantastic paper hats from tissue paper and trimmings—all give a festive feeling to those days of preparation.

A special present can be chosen for each individual on your gift list. For an avid gardener, what could be more useful than a sunbonnet to shield her on hot summer days? A homemade band box, filled with potpourri, has a delicious scent that immediately brings the warmth of summer to even the coldest winter day. Originally, band boxes were used to hold hats, collars, and caps. They were most often larger boxes than those which we have pictured and described in this book. But our smaller boxes would be perfect containers for the hats, collars, and caps of a beloved doll. Or perhaps they might be used to store a hoard of beautiful buttons.

For a budding artist, our pinafore is ideal for protecting clothes from paint, spattered in moments of excessive creative fervor. The wool rabbit will fit in perfectly amid Christmas stocking plenty, or it can be tucked in among the jelly eggs in an Easter basket. Our pocket is designed for a person who is always misplacing sewing or other equipment. And the warmth of woolen mittens or slippers seems somehow increased when the objects are handmade and designed especially for the recipient.

The exclamations of delight and the looks of surprise on the faces of those who are fortunate enough to receive special, handmade presents are well worth the hours spent in making them, as well as the occasional headaches of trying to make something come out "just right."

Each idea presented in this book is meant only to give you an introduction to the procedures and methods for making the article.* Once you have made the basic project, the possibilities for personal innovations are limited only by your imagination. The personal touches you give your homemade gifts are what make them such treasures.

—*Tasha Tudor and Linda Allen*

*A Table of Metric Conversions and Equivalents is included at the back of the book.

Wool Rabbit

Materials

4 cardboard templates for body
  (see diagram)
cardboard for tail
fingering yarn, preferably wool
felt (for ears)
black beads or pieces of felt (for
  eyes)

horsehair or nylon thread (for
  whiskers)
strong string
needle
thread
pair of scissors
glue

1. Cut the templates out of stiff cardboard, otherwise they will bend when wound with the wool. Cut a 10″ length of strong string. Place it along the inner edge of a cardboard template, but leave some hanging

on each end in order to fasten the wool when the template is filled. Wind the yarn around the template evenly, in layers. Starting at one end of the template, wind to the other end and back again. Repeat this process until the template is full and there is no longer any indentation in the center of the semi-circle. Tie the string securely in the middle and clip off the winding yarn. Put a dab of glue along the inside edge, where the binding string is. This will help to secure the wool once it has been cut and trimmed. In this same way, fill both of the small and both of the large semi-circles.

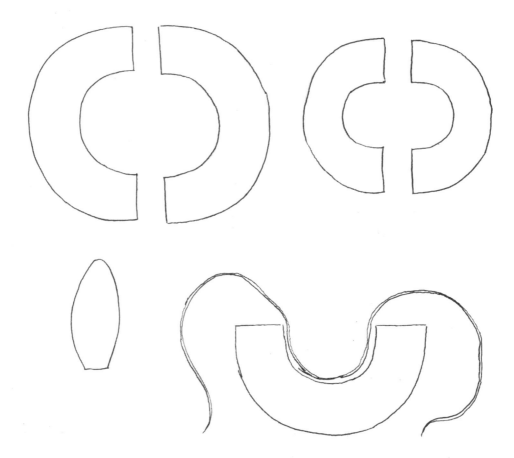

2. When both halves have been wound with the wool, tie the two small semi-circles together with the binding string to form a circle. Then do the same with the two large semi-circles.

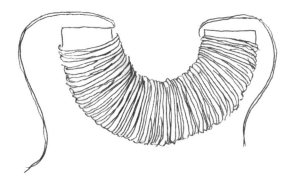

3. Cut the wool along the outside edge of the circles and remove the templates. Now cut another 10″ length of string and tie it securely around the center as an added protection against shedding.

4. To make the rabbit's tail, wrap yarn around a ½″ × 1½″ piece of cardboard about 100 times. Tie the wool in one place and cut. Trim into a round ball.

5. Now that the large and small balls and the tail have been completed, it's time to form the rabbit. Stitch the small ball to the large one. (The small ball is the head; the large one forms the body.) Sew the tail securely in place.

6. To make the figure look more rabbit-like, "sculpt" it with a pair of scissors. If necessary, look at an accurate picture that shows the configuration of a live rabbit. *No clipping should be done until the parts of the rabbit have been joined.*

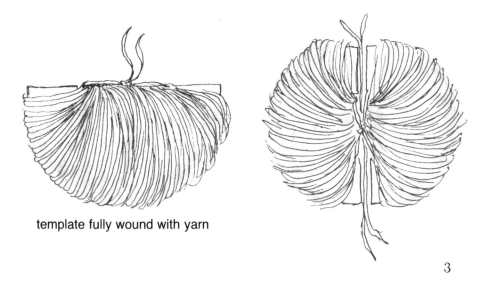

template fully wound with yarn

making the whiskers

assembled rabbit before trimming

7. Cut the ears from the felt and stitch in place. The eyes—either beads or felt—should be sewed firmly in place and should have the additional security of a dab of glue on each.

8. To attach the whiskers, thread a needle with a length of horsehair or nylon thread. Pass the needle through the rabbit's nose, from one side to the other, leaving about a 2″ piece to form a whisker. Pass the needle back to the side where you began and clip off a matching 2″ length of horsehair or nylon thread. Secure this set of whiskers with a dab of glue at the base of the loop end. Repeat this process until there are four sets of whiskers on each side of the rabbit's nose.

Note: The rabbit may be a solid color or a combination of two or more colors. By experimenting, you can discover different ways to wind the wool in order to make stripes or dots. If the rabbit is to be given to a small child, make very certain that all the parts are firmly fastened in place.

Doll's Band Box

Originally, band boxes were lined with newspaper, but you may use any lining you wish.

Materials

lightweight cardboard, such as
  the kind used for cracker
  boxes
paper printed with small designs
  or dollhouse wallpaper
paper to line the box
scissors

needle
sturdier needle to punch holes
thread
glue
tape measure
pencil

1. Cut out the cover, bottom, and side pieces according to diagram 1. The larger oval will form the top of the box cover; the smaller oval will be the bottom of the box. From the dollhouse wallpaper or small-figured paper, cut out cover and bottom pieces to correspond with the cardboard cover and bottom pieces. Cut the side pieces to fit the cardboard side pieces, with additional allowances of ¼″ on the top and bottom of each piece of paper, and an allowance of ¼″ on one end of the paper. These additional allowances will enable you to fold the paper over on the top and bottom edges; the extra ¼″ on one end of the paper will allow you to wrap the paper around the sides and overlap it a bit. Repeat this process for the lining paper.

2. With the sturdier needle, punch small holes at ¼″ intervals around the edge of the cardboard piece for the cover. Punch corresponding holes on the cardboard piece that will form the sides of the cover. Repeat this process for the cardboard pieces that will form the bottom

of the box. Sew the sides together, as indicated in diagram 2, making sure they fit snugly around the cover and bottom pieces.

3. Sew the cover top to the cover sides, using an overcast stitch. Be careful not to pull the stitches too tightly. Repeat this for the bottom of the box.

Diagram 1

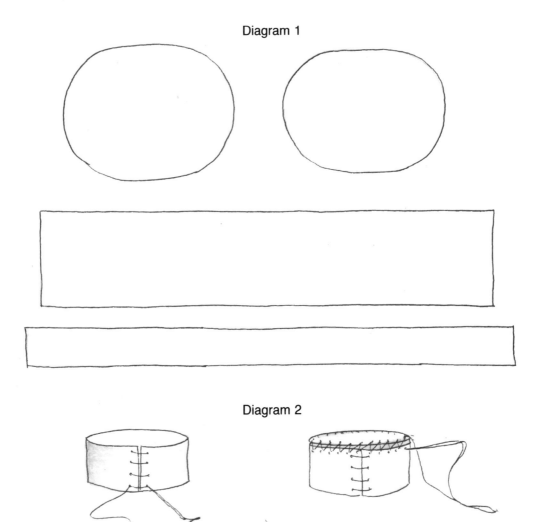

Diagram 2

Diagram 3

6

4. Now that the box is assembled, take the small-figured paper (cut to fit the side of the cover) and spread it generously with glue. Glue the paper to the sides of the cover. Clip around the upper and lower edges of the paper to facilitate turning, as indicated in diagram 3. Fold the edges over, onto the cover and the inside of the box. Take the piece of paper, cut to fit the cover top, and spread it with glue. Glue it to the top of the cover, concealing the folded-over edges of the side piece. Repeat this for the bottom of the box.

5. To line the box, repeat the same basic steps, gluing the inside of the cover top in place, then the sides. Do the same for the bottom of the box.

6. Once the box is put together, allow the pieces to dry somewhat. If they are put together before they are dry and if there are any bits of glue around the inside edge, you are liable to glue your box together and mar the paper when pulling the box apart.

Note: A band box can be made in any shape you wish. But when you cut out the top and bottom pieces, make sure that the top piece is slightly bigger than the bottom one.

Miniature Nesting Boxes

Nesting boxes intrigue both children and adults, and they are great fun to make. Follow the general directions given for constructing a band box (pp. 5-7), but increase the amount of materials (cardboard and paper).

1. Cut the top and bottom of the smallest box.

2. Cut the top and bottom of the next largest box. This should be just large enough to hold the smallest box when finished. If the smallest box has a bottom that measures ¾″ in diameter, the top must be slightly larger. The next box should have a bottom that measures 1⅛″ in diameter, with a slightly larger top. The next larger box should have a bottom measuring 1½″ in diameter, with a slightly larger top. The last box should have a bottom measuring 1⅞″ in diameter, with a slightly larger top.

Note: By following the above procedure, you can also make a set of larger nesting boxes.

the varying sizes for three
different shaped nesting box sets

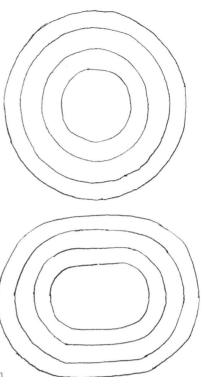

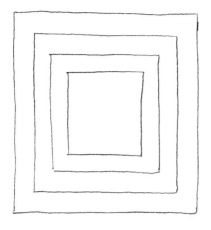

Cloth Book

For very young children, who often attempt to demolish the covers and paper pages of books, a cloth book is the answer. The book's contents are entirely up to the book-maker or the interests of the book's recipient. It could be an alphabet book or an animal book. Or you could make up your own story and illustrate it with your own pictures.

Materials

muslin or similar material for pages	felt (optional)
	scissors
wax crayons or indelible felt-tipped markers in assorted colors	pinking shears
	needle
	heavy-duty thread
calico, chintz, or brightly figured cotton for cover	white glue (optional)
	iron (optional)

1. Cut the cover out of the calico. Cut the inside muslin "pages" four times as long as the width you plan for the book, and about 1″ wider than the height of the book.

2. Lay the cloth pages on a flat surface. Fold in each end of each page to the middle, as shown in diagram 1. The page on the left will be the second page; the one under it will be the first page. The one to the right will be the next-to-last page; the one under it will be the last page.

3. Lay out all the pages. Each page will consist of a double thickness of cloth; the outer edge should be left uncut. The reason for this procedure is to prevent color and/or text from seeping through the cloth. The illustrations will be arranged so that the "wrong" side of the first page will back up against the "wrong" side of the second page. Both "wrong" sides will be hidden inside the folded cloth.

4. Flatten out the pages before drawing (or tracing) the text and the pictures on the muslin. Use permanent felt-tipped markers or wax crayons on only one side of the cloth. If you use crayons, press the letters and pictures with a warm, *not* hot, iron. The crayon markings will melt into the cloth and become almost as permanent as the fabric itself.

5. Reassemble the pages as described in step 2. Fold the book in the middle and sew along the spine, about ⅜″ in. Trim the top and bottom with pinking shears. For extra strength, sew down the spine once more.

6. The separate calico or chintz cover can now be stitched on. The cover can be decorated with cut-out felt letters (the title of the book or the name of the recipient) glued to the cloth. Or letters of solid-colored fabric can be appliquéd on the cover.

Diagram 1

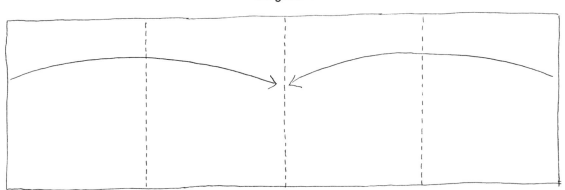

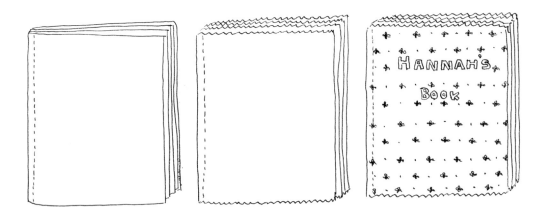

Child's Pinafore

The following directions are for a pinafore about 24″ long. Each square in the diagram equals 1″. For a larger or smaller size, change the size that the squares in the diagram represent.

Materials

1⅓ yards of cotton fabric
matching thread
folded-over bias tape (measuring
  ½″ when folded)*
3 buttons, ¾″ in diameter
rick-rack or ribbon trim (optional)

scissors
needle
pins
tape measure
iron

1. Cut out the front and back pieces according to the diagram. With right sides together, pin the front piece to the back at the shoulder and side seams.

Diagram 1

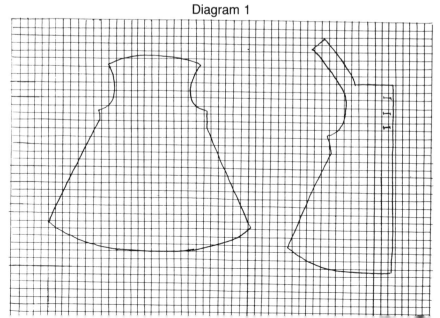

2. Stitch the seams and press them open.

3. With bias tape or bias strips, bind the armholes, neck opening, and the opening in the back of the pinafore. Also bind the bottom edge of the pinafore.

4. Make three buttonholes to fit the ¾″ buttons at the places indicated in the diagram. Sew on the buttons. Press. The pinafore may be further decorated with trimming, such as rick-rack or embroidered ribbon.

*Instead of bias tape, you can cut bias strips of the pinafore fabric to bind the edges. This will require an extra amount of fabric.

Stuffed Dog

Materials

¼ yard of natural-colored, strong cotton fabric
black velveteen for trimming
cotton or synthetic stuffing
2 black shank buttons, approximately ¼" in diameter
black embroidery floss
scissors
needle
thread

1. From the cotton fabric, cut the main body piece, A, and two pieces B for the stomach. Follow diagram 1 for the pattern shapes. From the black velveteen, cut one piece C for the top of the dog's head; four pieces D for the ears; and two pieces E for the tail.

2. With right sides together, match pieces A and B and stitch them together, as shown in diagram 2. Stitch one of the tail pieces, E, to each of the A pieces at point a, as indicated in diagram 2. Stitch piece C to one of the A pieces, as shown in diagram 3. With right sides together, stitch together the two body halves, as shown in diagram 4. Leave a 4" opening on the dog's stomach to allow for stuffing.

3. Turn the dog right side out and stuff him with cotton or synthetic stuffing. The stuffing should be firm, but not lumpy. Make certain the dog's tail is also stuffed. Stitch the opening for the stuffing.

4. Place two D (ear) pieces right sides together and sew around the rounded edges, as shown in diagram 5. Repeat this step with the other two ear pieces. Turn them right side out. Turn in the bottom raw edge not quite ¼". Close the ear with slipstitches. Sew the finished ears firmly in place, as shown in diagram 6. Sew on the two black buttons for the eyes. (If you plan to give the dog to a child, the buttons should be firmly and carefully sewn on so that they won't come off.)

Diagram 1   3 squares = 1 inch

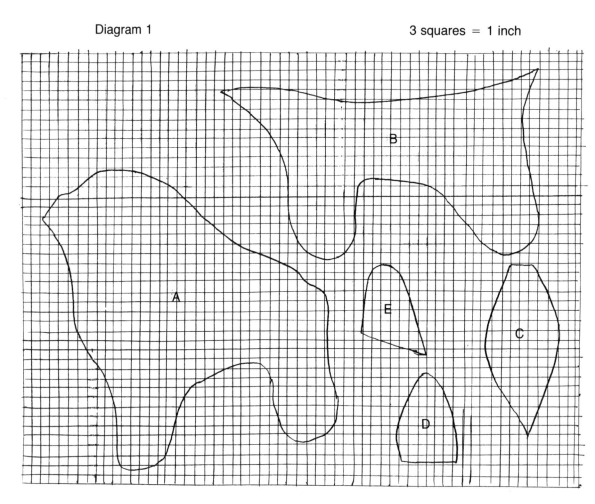

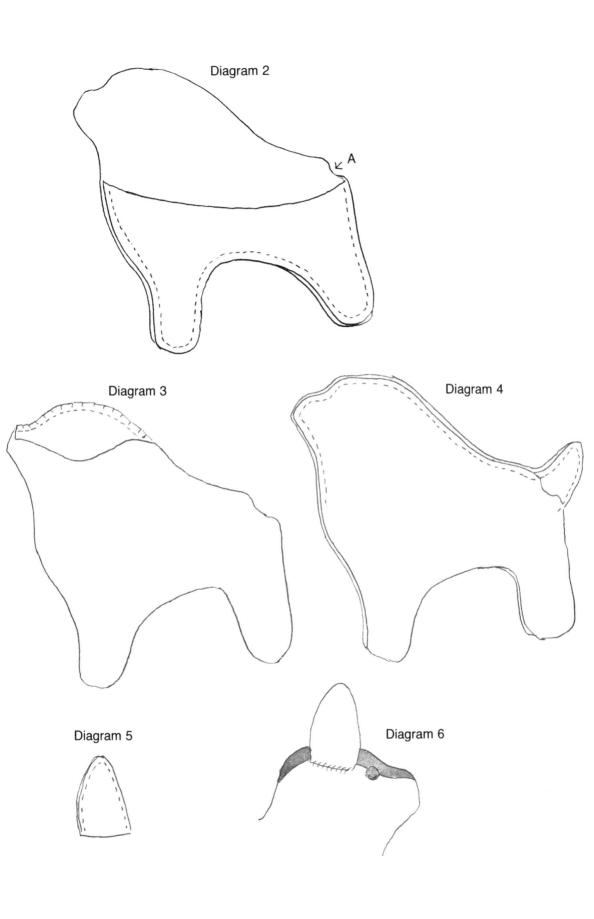

Diagram 2

A

Diagram 3

Diagram 4

Diagram 5

Diagram 6

5. Thread a needle with four strands of black embroidery thread and fill in the space for the nose by sewing over and over, as shown in diagram

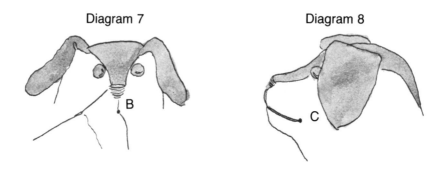

7. Without cutting the thread, bring it to point b, directly below the dog's nose. Insert the needle there and bring the thread back up to the base of the nose. Again, insert the needle and thread at point b and bring it out at point c, on the side of the face below the eye. Bring the needle and thread back to the center, insert the needle, and again bring the thread out at point c. Repeat this last step once more. Then repeat the entire process for the other side of the mouth (see diagram 8).

Sunbonnet

The following instructions are for a woman's bonnet. For a smaller bonnet, reduce the size according to the graph squares on the pattern. We have used a gauge of one square to 1″. All of the seam allowances are ¼″ unless otherwise stated.

Materials

1 yard of calico or similar cotton, at least 36" wide

⅓ yard of stiffening

15 shirt buttons, approximately
  ⅓" in diameter

1 yard of ½" twill tape

scissors

tape measure

pins

needle

thread

iron

1. Cut out piece A, the two brim pieces, B, and the two tie strings, C, as shown in diagram 1. Cut a third brim piece out of the stiffening material. Cut and piece bias strips of the cotton fabric for enclosing the back edge of the brim and the outside edge of the main body of the bonnet. These strips should be 1¼" wide. The strip that encloses the top edge of the bonnet body should be 1¾" wide.

Diagram 1

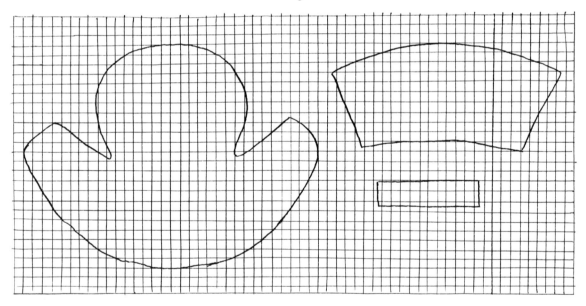

2. Baste the stiffening onto the wrong side of one of the brim pieces. With right sides together, sew the two bonnet brim pieces, starting at point a and ending at point b, as shown in the diagram. Grade the seam

Diagram 2

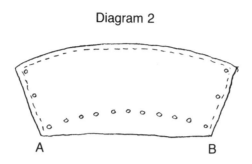

A   B

allowance, then turn right side out and press. Topstitch the brim as indicated in diagram 2, or make your own topstitch design.

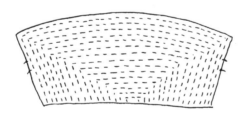

3. Take a 1¼" bias strip to fit the back, unsewn edge of the brim. With right sides together, stitch this to the top side of the brim. Turn the strip over, enclosing the raw edge of the brim, and press. On the underside of the brim, turn over the unsewn edge of the bias strip and pin in place. Turn in the ends of the strip and stitch them in place as you do so.

Diagram 3

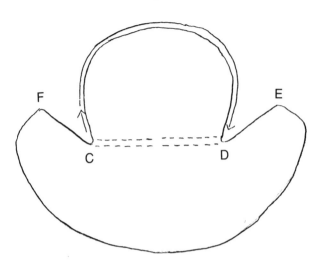

4. Next, prepare the two string pieces. On each piece, hem over all four edges, using a ⅜" allowance. Hand sew these at the points indicated in diagram 2. Sew on the buttons at the indicated points.

5. Cut the bias 1¾" strip to fit for the top edge of the bonnet body. Cut two straight strips to fit across the neck of the bonnet body; these will form a casing for the drawstring that will make the bonnet fit well at the back of the head. The strips should each be 8" long (to allow for turning over the raw edges at each end) and 1¼" wide.

6. Starting at point c, sew the bias strip on the top edge of the bonnet body, ending at point d. Next, sew some of the narrower bias strips from point d to point e, and point f to c. Along the bottom edge of the bonnet, sew the narrower bias strip from point f to point e. Turn all of these over ½" and hem in place. Press. Take the two strips cut to form the drawstring casing and press over all edges ¼". Sew these in place along the lines indicated in diagram 3 and along the top and bottom edges. Press the casings after they have been sewn in place. Cut two strips of twill tape, each 10" long. Insert these through the casings and fasten the ends securely at the outside edges (points c and d). At the

same time, close up the casings at points c and d. The other two ends will meet in the middle so that the material can be drawn together and tied when properly gathered. At the places indicated in diagram 4, make buttonholes to fit the buttons.

7. Button together the two pieces—brim and bonnet body. Gather the drawstring to fit the back of the head comfortably.

Diagram 4

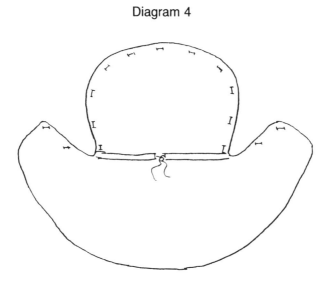

Note: Whenever it is necessary to iron the bonnet, unbutton the two pieces and iron them separately.

Pocket

Materials

⅓ yard of calico, percale, or similar fabric	scissors
	pins
⅓ yard of fabric for lining	needle
bias tape	thread
grosgrain ribbon or cord	tape measure

1. Cut out the pocket and the lining pieces, as shown in diagram 1.

front of pocket
and front lining   back and back lining

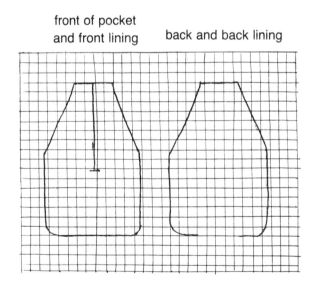

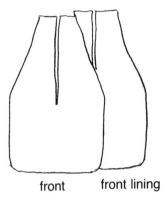

front   front lining

2. Baste together the front pocket and front lining (with the wrong sides together). Do the same with the back of the pocket and the back lining.

back lining

back

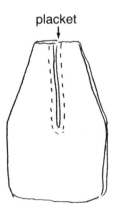

placket

3. Bind the placket opening on the front with bias tape.

4. Pin the front and back sections, lining sides together, in place and baste around the outer edges. Bind the edges with bias tape except for the top edge, where the waist cord will be, as shown in the diagram.

5. Cut a straight strip of either the lining or the main fabric to bind the upper edge. The strip should be 1½″ wide, and the length should be the same as that of the top of the pocket plus ⅝″ allowance on either end for turnover. Baste this strip in place, enclosing the raw edge. Topstitch the basted strip in place, from one side to the other, through all layers. Leave the ends, with the ⅝″ allowance, open to allow for the insertion of the waist cords.

6. The waist cords can be made with either grosgrain ribbon or long cords. The cords can be braided to the desired length. Whichever type of cord you choose, the cord for the left side of the pocket should be about 18″ longer than that for the right side. When the pocket is worn, the tie should be on the right side (unless the wearer is left-handed). The length of these cords depends on the girth of the pocket-wearer. When the waist cords have been cut to the proper length, fasten them into the open ends of the binding strip. Sew down the edges of the strip and press the pocket.

baste the front and back together and bind with bias tape

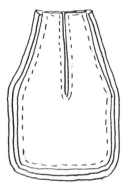 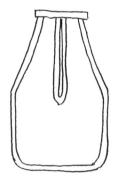

Patterned Mittens

The directions we have given are for an average-size woman's mitten. For a man's size, use worsted yarn. For a child's mitten, use fingering yarn and #2 knitting needles.

The colors are left to your discretion. Often, combinations of red and white, blue and white, grey and white, black and grey, red and black, green and red are used. But this will be up to you.

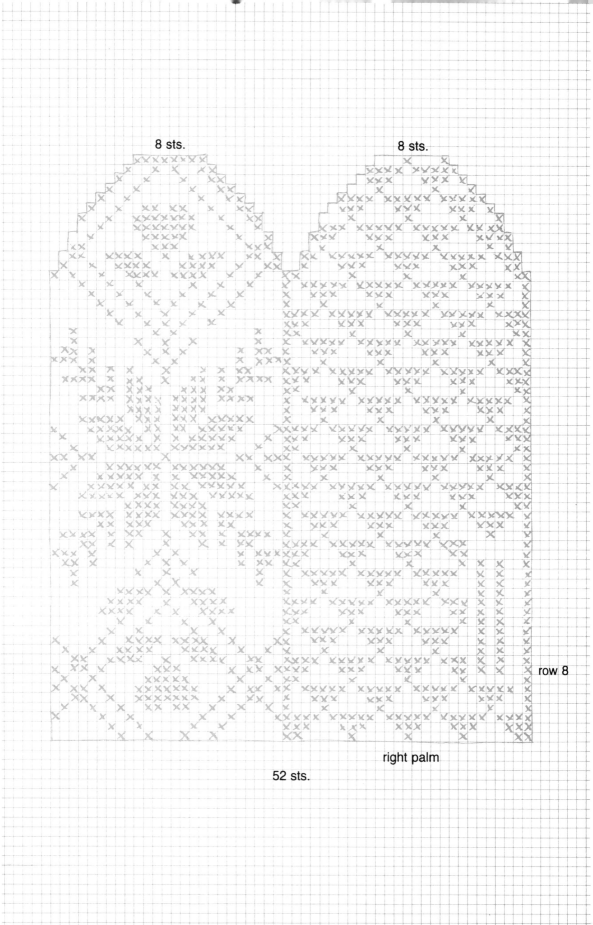

8 sts.

8 sts.

row 8

right palm

52 sts.

Materials

3 ounces of sport yarn for the background color

3 ounces of sport yarn for the pattern color

1 set of #3 7" double-pointed knitting needles

stitch holder

The knitting gauge should be 7 stitches to the inch.

If you have never done any pattern knitting before, there are a few facts you should know before you begin:

The pattern should be read from right to left.

Each square in this pattern represents one stitch.

When it is time to add on the pattern color, do not tie it on. Leave an end, about 4" long, loose. After the piece is completed, these ends may be fastened in with a darning needle on the wrong side.

As you knit, carry the yarn not in use along the back side of the work, being careful not to pull it tight. To carry the yarn, twist the yarn to be carried around the yarn you are using. A maximum of four stitches should be taken without carrying the yarn in this fashion.

Don't break the yarn unless it is no longer in the pattern.

1. FOR THE RIGHT MITTEN, cast on 52 stitches with the background color yarn. Divide these stitches onto three needles. Work in K 1, P 1 ribbing for 3½". Knit one row. The pattern begins in the next row. Reading from right to left: K 2 in the pattern color; K 5 in the background color (remember to carry the pattern color along on the back). K 1 in pattern color; K 5 in background color; K 1 in pattern; K 5 in background, and so on, until you reach the end of the first pattern round. Continue to follow the diagram until you reach row 8.

2. In row 8, the base of the thumb gusset is begun. In this row, knit as follows: K 1 in the pattern color; K 2 in the background color; K 1 in the

thumb   left palm

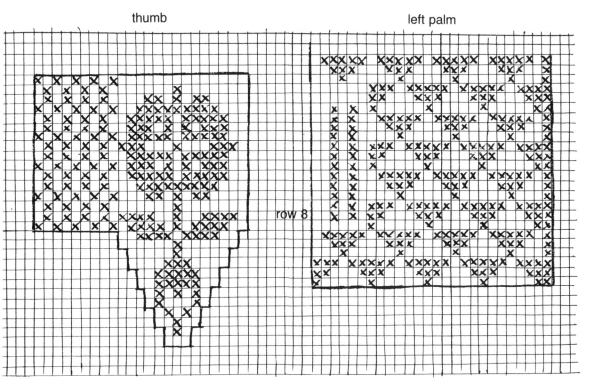

row 8

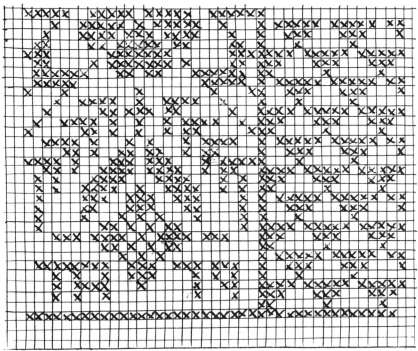

an example of initials and year date inserted into the design

pattern; increase 1 stitch; K 1 in the background color. Make another increase; K 1 in the pattern; and then continue to follow the diagram to the end of the round. The two pattern stitches outside the increase mark will be the outline of the thumb gusset. Every other row, these increases will be repeated inside these outline stitches. After each increase round, there will be two more stitches for the thumb. When you have 13 stitches for the thumb, you will be at row 19 on the diagram.

3. In row 20, slip the 13 thumb stitches onto a stitch holder. Cast on 5 stitches over these and finish the row. In row 21, K 2 together twice over these 5 stitches. You will once again have 52 stitches on the needles.

4. Continue to follow the pattern diagram until you are ready to decrease for the tip of the mitten. Then divide the stitches so that there are 26 stitches on one needle (this will be the palm needle); 13 on the second needle, and 13 on the third needle (these are for the back of the mitten).

5. Working in the pattern, begin decreasing as follows:

on the first needle: K 1; slip 1; K 1; pass slip stitch over knit stitch; knit to within the last three stitches on needle; K 2 together, K 1.

the second needle: K 1; slip 1; K 1; pass slip stitch over knit stitch; K to the end of the needle.

the third needle: K to within the last three stitches on the needle; K 2 together, K 1.
K one round.

Repeat these two rows for three more decreasing rounds, then begin decreasing in every row until there are only 8 stitches for the palm and 8 stitches for the back of the mitten. Break the yarn, leaving about 9″ of the background and pattern colors. Run these ends through the 16 stitches and fasten securely.

6. To finish the thumb, slip the 15 stitches for the thumb from the

holder onto two of the needles. Pick up and K 8 stitches over the 5 stitches cast on. Divide these 23 stitches onto three needles and join. Knit around and around, following the diagram for the pattern. When the pattern is finished, break the pattern color, leaving an end long

sample pattern for mittens with space for initials and date

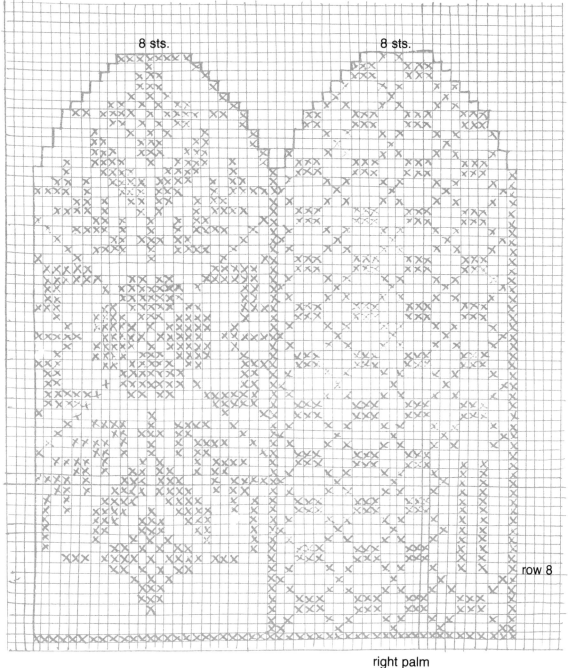

right palm

52 sts.

enough to fasten in later. Continue in the background color, and decrease for the tip as follows: K 2 together; K 1; repeat until only six stitches are left. Break off the yarn, leaving about 6–7″. Run this yarn through the stitches and fasten securely.

7. FOR THE LEFT MITTEN, begin the same way you did for the right mitten, but when you reach the pattern, follow the diagram for the left-hand palm and thumb gusset. When the gusset is completed, put these 15 stitches on a holder and continue to follow the diagrams for the right hand.

Note: We have given you a specific pattern to follow, but you might like to create your own designs. Simply take a piece of graph paper, keeping in mind that one square equals 1″, and mark the outline of the mitten on the paper. Divide the outline into the palm and back of the mitten, as shown previously. Then use your imagination and create patterns to fit inside the diagram, such as birds, flowers, or geometric designs. If you wish, you can further personalize the design by including the initials of the person who will receive the mittens. Or you might like to include your own initials and the date when the mittens were made.

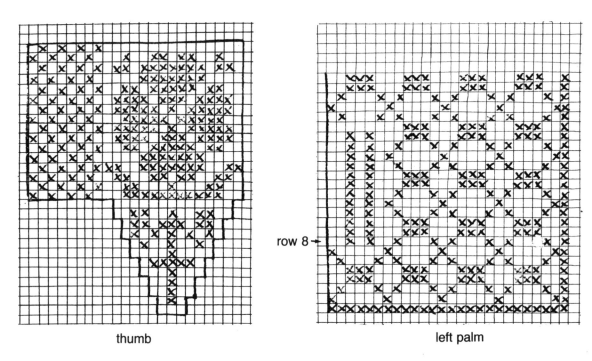

thumb

row 8 →

left palm

34

Patchwork Potholders

Ideally, the fabrics you choose for your patchwork pieces should be those with small patterns. Or, if you prefer, you can alternate printed fabrics with plain colored ones. They should be shirt-weight cotton. If heavier, they will be difficult to turn at the corners; if lighter, there will be problems with puckering. All the fabric pieces should be of equal weight. Many old pieces of fabric have beautiful designs, but if you want an item that will last longer, we suggest that you use new fabric. New fabric should be washed before using in order to test it for colorfastness and shrinkage. After it has been washed and dried, it should be pressed. We have provided instructions for a square (8" × 8") and an octagonal potholder. But you can easily make larger or smaller ones.

Materials

a selection of fabrics
backing fabric, 8½" × 8½"
cardboard for templates
cotton or synthetic quilt batting
bias tape

small curtain ring
scissors
needle
thread
iron

Square Potholder

1. Following the shapes in diagram 1, cut out the cardboard templates. For this design, you will need three different fabrics, and there should be enough of one of them for the 8½" × 8½" backing piece as well as for the pieces using the templates. The three different kinds of fabrics will be designated as A, B, and C. Cut eight small triangles of fabric A. The templates allow for a ¼" turnover allowance. Cut four triangles, plus the backing square, out of fabric B. Then cut five squares and four triangles out of fabric C.

2. When joining the pieces, the basic idea is to join the smallest to the smallest, and then the larger to the larger until the finished block is

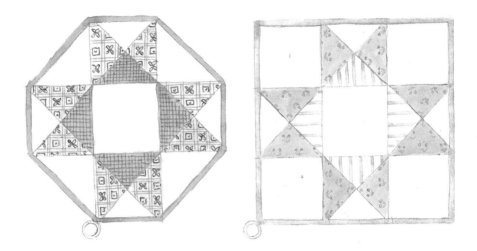

formed. As each piece is sewn to another, the seam should be pressed to one side. This will cause the fabric to lie flat, and there will be no problem with puckers when it is sewn to another piece.

3. Following the pattern in diagram 2, join the two small triangular pieces to form a large triangle, using tiny running stitches. An A and a

Diagram 1

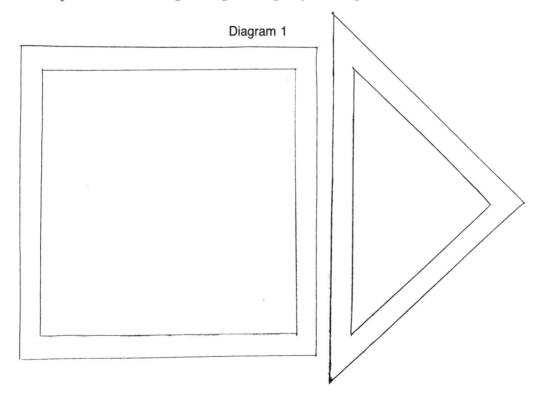

B triangle are then sewn together to form a large triangle. Repeat this step with all of the B pieces. This will make four large triangles, each consisting of one A and one B triangle. Next, use one A and one C triangle and repeat the same step. Now you have four more larger triangles, each consisting of one A and one C triangle. Sew two of these triangles together to form a square. Each square will include an A–B and an A–C triangle. When you have finished joining the triangles, you will have four patterned squares. The design is composed of three straight strips; each strip is composed of three squares. The first strip has a C square, then a patterned square, then another C square. The second strip has a patterned square, then a C square, then another patterned square. The third strip is made by following the same sequence as the first square. Sew these blocks together to form the strips. Then sew the strips together, in the order given, to make the finished block. Remember that after each seam is sewn, it must be pressed so that the finished block will be even and neat in appearance.

4. Cut a piece of the quilt batting to fit the square. Then place the batting on the wrong side of the patchwork piece. Place the backing behind the batting piece, with the wrong side to the batting. This forms a sandwich: patchwork square, batting, and backing. Baste these three pieces together close to the edges. Cut a strip of the bias tape and bind all four edges of the potholder. For hanging, attach a small curtain ring to one corner of the finished potholder.

Diagram 2

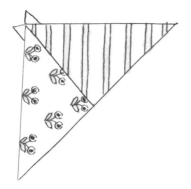 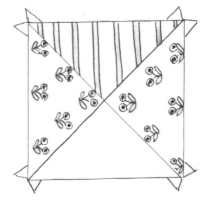

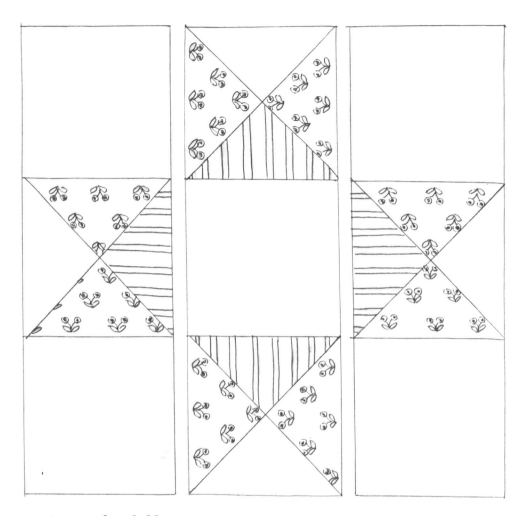

Octagonal Potholder

By using the same basic design for the square potholder, you can make an octagonal one. Cut out only three pieces for the templates. Take two square pieces, and cut each of them across the middle, from one corner to the other, to form two pairs of matching triangles. When sewing the strips together, use the following format: one large C triangle, one patterned square, one large triangle. The second strip should be the same as that of the A, C, and a pattern for the square potholder. The third strip should repeat the first—a large triangle, a patterned square, and another triangle. These strips should then be sewn together, sandwiched, basted, and bound in the same way as the square potholder.

Patterned Slipper-Socks

The following directions are for an average-sized pair of women's slippers. Use finer yarn to make a pair of children's slippers, and heavier yarn to make a pair of men's slippers.

If you would like to create your own design, outline the shape of the slipper-sock on graph paper and fill in your own pattern on the graph squares.

Materials

3 ounces of knitting worsted for background color

3 ounces of knitting worsted for pattern color

1 set of #3 double-pointed knitting needles

1 pair of sock soles (women's 9–10")

1. The knitting gauge is 7 stitches to the inch. Starting with the background color, cast on 58 stitches. Divide these onto three needles, join and work in K 1, P 1 ribbing for four rows. Knit one row, then divide the stitches so that there are 29 (for the instep) on two of the needles, and 29 (for the heel) on one needle.

2. To reinforce the heel, work as follows: K 1; slip 1 across the row; P back. Repeat these two rows until there are 16 rows on the heel, ending with the purl row. Turn the heel. Beginning on the purl row, P 16; P 2 together; P 1; turn. Slip 1; K 4; K 2 together; K 1; turn. Slip 1; P 5; P 2 together; P 1; turn. Slip 1; K 6; K 2 together; K 1; turn. Continue to work in this way by having one more stitch before the decrease on each row until 17 stitches are left. With the right side of the work facing you, K 9 on the left side of the heel. K 29 heel stitches onto one needle. Pick up and K 9 on the right side of the heel, and knit to the center of the heel. Divide the 35 stitches you now have for the heel onto two needles.

3. For the heel gusset, begin at the heel center. Knit to within three stitches at the end of the needle; K 2 together, K 1. K across the 29 instep stitches. On the last needle; K 1; K 2 together; K to the end of the needle. Continue this decrease for two more rows. You once again

40

have 29 stitches for the heel and 29 stitches for the instep. At this point, you will begin to knit the pattern. Beginning on the instep needle, reading from right to left, knit around and around, following the pattern diagram. On row 37, the decrease for the toe begins. Working in the pattern, knit as follows:

instep needle: K 1, slip 1, K 1. Pass slip stitch over the knit stitch. K to within the last three stitches on the needle; K 2 together; K 1.

first sole needle: K 1, slip 1, K 1. Pass slip stitch over knit stitch. K to the end of the needle.

second sole needle: K to within the last three stitches on the needle; K 2 together; K 1.

K one row.

Repeat these two rounds until 15 stitches remain for the sole and 15 stitches for the instep. Break the yarn, leaving about a 15″ end of the main (background) color and enough of the pattern color to fasten off later.

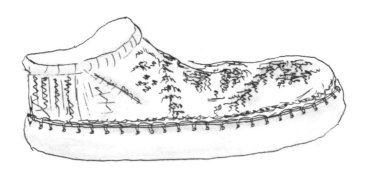

4. Join the toe as follows: Place the instep stitches on one needle and the sole stitches on the second needle; insert the 15″ length of yarn into a darning needle. Beginning with the yarn attached to the back needle,* pass the needle through the first stitch on the front needle as if to knit. Slip the stitch off the needle. Then pass it through the next stitch as if to purl, but leave the stitch on the knitting needle. Pass the needle and yarn through the first stitch on the back needle as if to purl. Slip this stitch off. Pass the yarn and needle through the second stitch on the back needle as if to knit, but leave the stitch on the knitting needle. ** Repeat this from * to ** until all the stitches are woven together. Fasten off the yarn. Care must be used so that the tension of the woven stitches matches that of the knitted ones. Both the socks are made in the same way. Press the slippers.

5. To attach the soles, pin the heel of each slipper to the heel of each sole, matching the center backs. Do the same at the toe. Baste the sole to the sock, following the pattern outline, except at the gusset, where the outline comes slightly above the sole. With the needle and double strand of yarn, sew together with blanket stitches. Remove the basting stitches.

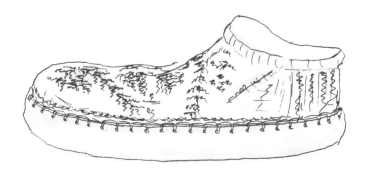

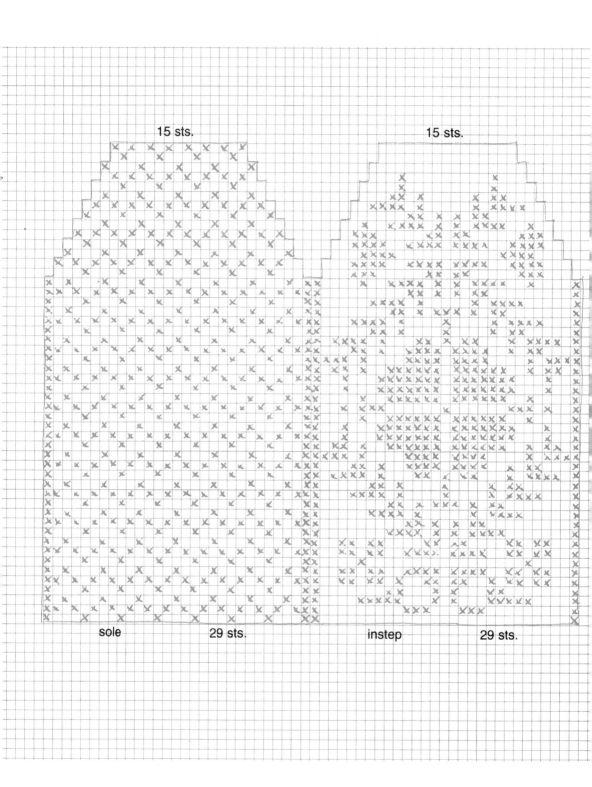

15 sts.　　　　　　　　　　　15 sts.

sole　　　　29 sts.　　　　instep　　　　29 sts.

44

sample slipper design with initials and date

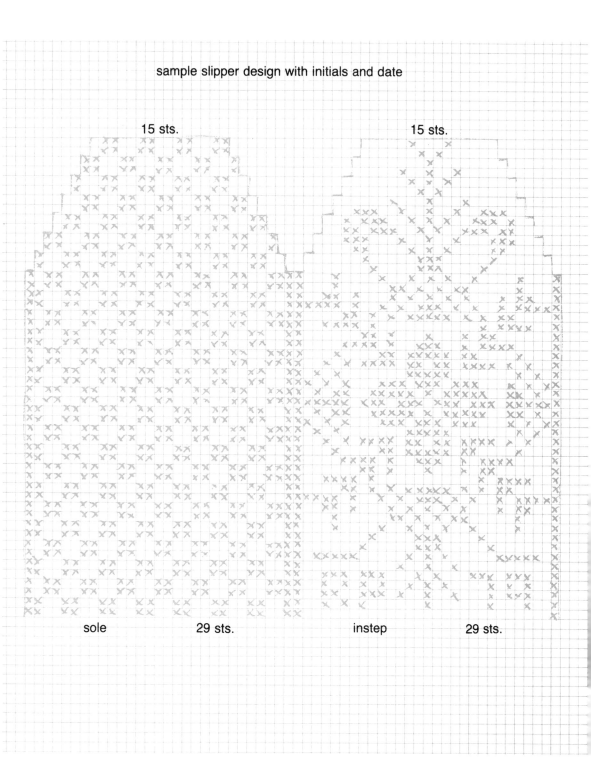

15 sts.   15 sts.

sole   29 sts.   instep   29 sts.

Paper Hats and Crowns

Depending on the occasion, paper hats can be made of white or colored tissue paper, crepe paper, foil paper, or colored printed wrapping paper. For a stronger tissue-paper hat, it is best to use a double layer.

Plain Paper Hat

Materials
large sheets of tissue paper,   scissors
   each approximately 24″ × 18″   glue
plain colored wrapping paper

1. Take two sheets of tissue paper and fold them in half, as shown in diagram 1. Next, take the upper corners (first the left and then the right) and fold them down to meet at point a, as shown in diagram 2. Crease the folds. Take the bottom edge of the layered sheets on the top side and fold it against the body of the hat, as shown in diagram 3. Repeat this process for the other side of the hat.

2. When opened out at the bottom edge, you will have a very simple hat that can be decorated with paper feathers and/or designs cut out of colored wrapping paper.

Robin Hood Hat

Materials
(see Plain Paper Hat)

1. Hold a plain paper hat so that one of the points is facing you. Gently flatten the hat by pulling out the sides and folding the front and back points together at the bottom, as shown in diagram 4. Take the bottom point, b, and fold it up to point c, as shown in diagram 5.

2. Open up the hat. Cut feather shapes out of wrapping paper and glue them to the body of the hat.

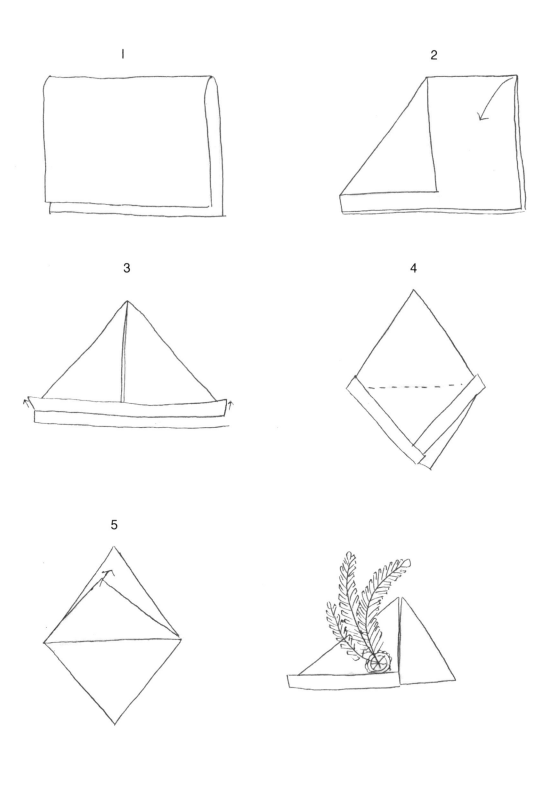

1

2

3

4

5

Medieval or Sorcerer's Hat

You can make either a medieval maiden's hat with long streamers or you can make a sorcerer's hat with cut-out symbols and mystical shapes glued to the body of the hat. The hat's basic shape is conical.

Materials

tissue paper sheets, each ap-
    proximately 24" × 18"
colored crepe paper or foil pa-
    per

ribbons (optional)
scissors
glue
gummed tape or stapler

1. Take two sheets of tissue paper and roll them into a cone by bringing point a to point b, as shown in diagram 1. Spread a little glue along the inside edge c–d and secure the paper in a conical shape. Trim the bottom edge of the cone so that it is even all around.

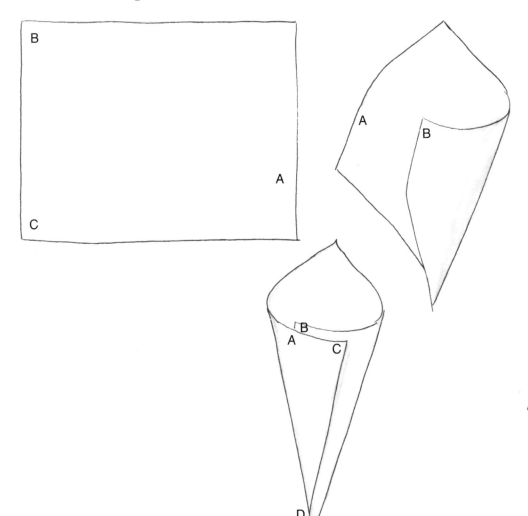

2. Cut long streamers out of colored crepe paper or foil paper (or use ribbons). Make sure that the streamers are longer than the bottom edge of the hat. The streamers can also be cut in varying lengths or they can be fringed to create a particularly dazzling effect. Fasten the streamers to the top of the hat with tape or staples.

3. Trim the bottom edge of the hat by gluing on a strip of colored crepe paper or foil paper.

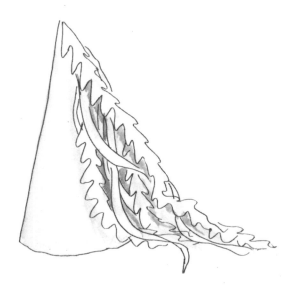

Note: For a sorcerer's hat, omit the streamers. Cut various shapes, such as moons, stars, or zodiac signs, out of foil paper and glue them onto the hat.

Paper Crown
For a truly regal crown, it is best to use gold or silver foil wrapping paper. If the paper is too flimsy, you can obtain the desired sturdiness by gluing two layers of the paper together with white glue.

Materials
gold or silver foil wrapping
 paper
colored foil papers (optional)

finely pointed scissors
glue or stapler
pencil

50

1. Cut a strip of the foil paper long enough to fit around the wearer's head. It should be 5″ high and should allow for a 1″ overlap. Fold the foil paper in half twice. With a pencil, lightly mark the cut-out designs for the crown (see diagram 1). If the pencil does not write on the foil paper, it will make a slight indentation you can follow. The shaded areas in the diagram indicate which parts of the foil paper will be cut out. However, you could also create your own designs. Cut out the designs with a pair of finely pointed scissors.

2. Carefully unfold the hat and smooth out the creases as much as possible. With a stapler or with glue, fasten the crown together at points a and b.

Diagram 1

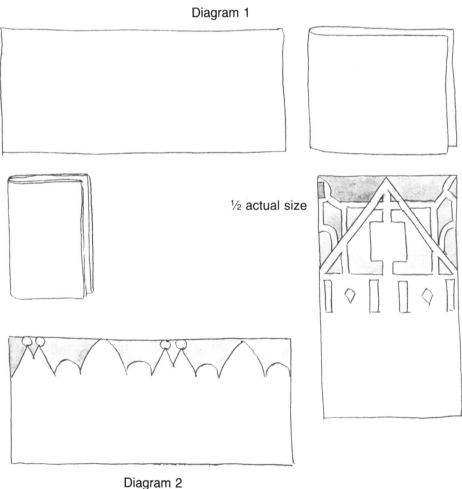

½ actual size

Diagram 2
¼ actual size

Note: If you don't want a cut-out crown, cut the crown strip, but instead of folding it cut a simple design along the top edge, as shown in diagram 2. You can use various colored foil papers—red, green, and blue, for example—and cut "jewels" out of them. Glue the pieces on the crown. Finish the crown according to the directions given for the cut-out crown.

Patchwork Pillow

The procedure for making the patchwork design for this pillow is basically the same as that given for the patchwork potholders (pp. 35-39). The pillow pattern is composed of small pieces joined together to form larger pieces. This design is made up of blocks, instead of strips, like those used for the potholder. Be sure to press each seam after it has been sewn.

Materials

Fabrics in four colors
   color A: ⅛ yard
   color B: ⅛ yard
   color C: ⅛ yard
   color D: ½ yard
cardboard for templates
cotton or synthetic pillow stuffing

scissors
tape measure
needle
thread
iron

1. Cut out the templates according to the designs in diagram 1. Then cut out the following pieces: eight triangles of color A; sixteen triangles of color B; two rhomboids of color C; two rhomboids of color D; one 12½" × 13½" backing square; two 3" × 13½" strips, and two 3" × 8½" strips, all of color D.

2. The design for the pillow consists of four squares; each square is made up of two strips. To make the squares, sew together one triangle A and one triangle B. Repeat this step to make another square. Sew the two squares together to make a strip, as shown in diagram 2. Make the second strip with two of the B triangles and one of the C rhomboids. Then sew the two strips, with long sides together, to form a larger square of about 4" × 4". Make another square by repeating this step. To make the other two squares, repeat the process, but use a D rhomboid instead of a C rhomboid. Take one square of each of the two designs and sew them together, as shown in diagram 3. Do the same with the other two squares. Match the middle seams of the two strips and sew them together to form a large square, like the block shown in the diagram.

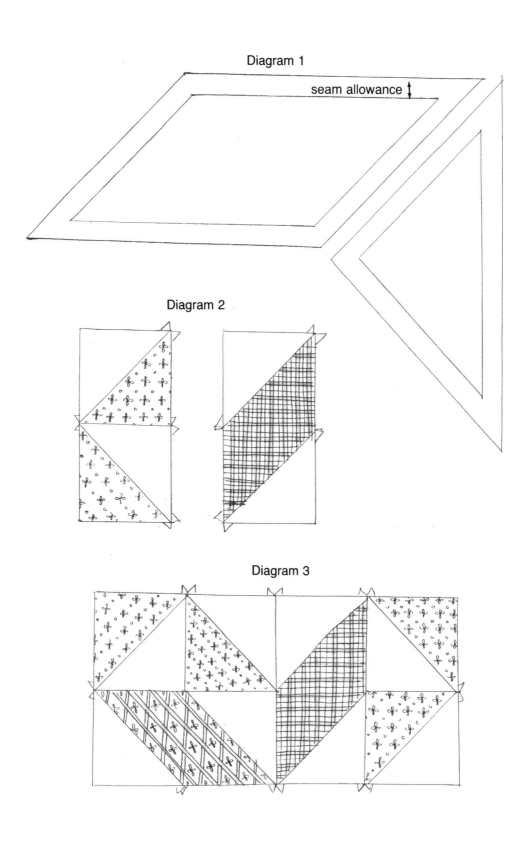

Diagram 1

seam allowance

Diagram 2

Diagram 3

3. To complete the top of the pillow, take the two 3″ × 8½″ strips and sew each along the opposite sides of the patchwork square. This gives you a rectangular piece. Take the other two 3″ × 13½″ strips and sew one each to the long sides of the rectangle. The patchwork design should be surrounded by a border of color D. Place the 13½″ × 13½″ backing square (color D) on top of the patchwork piece, right sides together. Sew around three sides. Turn right side out and press. Stuff with pillow stuffing, and close the fourth side with slipstitching.

Potpourri

Materials

any 6 or more of the following
dried materials:
rose petals, rose buds, lavender, orange peel, lemon
peel, vetiver root, cinnamon
sticks, cloves, rose geranium
leaves, lemon verbena leaves

essential oil of your choice (rose,
lemon verbena, oak moss, etc.)*
wire or mesh screens
dry, clean crock or jar with
cover

1. Gather your fresh scenting materials on a clear, dry day. Pick rose petals when they are truly fresh. Ideally, you should use the petals and buds from beautifully scented, old-fashioned roses because they will give your potpourri a more delicious scent. But, if necessary, modern tea roses may be substituted. At the same time you pick the roses, pluck rose geranium and lemon verbena leaves, as well as lavender spikes. The flowers at the tops of the spikes should still be in bud. Don't wait until the flowers are fully opened.

*available in drugstores and health food shops

2. Spread all the ingredients on screens in a hot, dry place (such as an attic), away from direct light. Turn the ingredients every day until they are thoroughly dry. *It is very important that the ingredients are absolutely dry*—a process that usually takes several weeks.

3. Combine the dry ingredients in a crock. Stir well. Add cinnamon sticks, vetiver root, and dried orange and lemon peels stuck with cloves (insert the cloves in the peels before the peels are dry). Then add a few drops of essential oil. Be sparing with the oil because it is very potent. Too much of it will ruin the potpourri. Stir the contents thoroughly, then cover the crock. Stir the potpourri every few days for several weeks before using.

Sachets

Aromatic sachets do wonders to help keep enclosed places—bureau drawers, closets, storage boxes, and trunks—smelling delightfully fresh and clean. The choice of scent you use is up to you. You might prefer a potpourri of which you are particularly fond, or you might like to fill the sachets with a particular flower or herbal scent. Many of the ingredients for filling sachets can be grown in a home garden or in windowsill pots. But if you don't have a garden or a green thumb, you can buy many of the ingredients. Most health food stores carry dried herbs and roots, and there is also a wide range of shops that stock herb products.

Materials for 1 Sachet

9″ piece of taffeta or satin ribbon, 3″ wide, or a 9″ × 4″
     piece of satin or taffeta fabric
potpourri, aromatic herbs, or
   roots

½ yard of ¼″ ribbon
scissors
needle
thread

1. Fold the 9″ ribbon or the 9″ × 4″ piece of fabric in half, as shown in diagram 1. If you are using fabric, fold the piece with right sides together and stitch a ½″ seam allowance on each of the longer edges. Then turn the material right side out and press. If you are using ribbon, stitch it with the right sides together, but instead of a ½″ seam allowance, stitch the ribbon along the very edge. (Since this is not a cut edge, there is no need for a seam allowance to prevent raveling problems.) You now have formed a little bag.

Diagram 1

Note: A wide selection of excellent quality dried herbs, roots, petals, and fragrance oils is available from Caswell-Massey & Company, Ltd. Their mail-order address is 575 Lexington Avenue, New York, N.Y. 10022. For a nominal fee, they will also send a catalog describing their many products.

2. Put some of your chosen scenting material into the bag. Pack the filling very loosely, otherwise the bag will be too full to tie with ribbon. Turn in the top edges about ¼″ and stitch the bag closed. With the ½ yard of ¼″ ribbon, tie the bag in the middle, as shown in diagram 2, or at the top, as shown in diagram 3.

Diagram 2

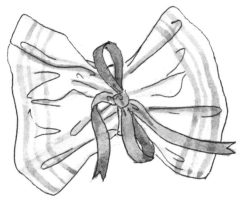

Diagram 3

Holiday or Birthday Snappers

Snappers are especially fun to have at birthday parties or at Christmastime. A snapper, made especially for each person, can be placed at each table setting. Or snappers can even be used as Christmas tree decorations, to be taken down and opened, with other Christmas presents.

Materials

cardboard tubes, such as those
   used for gift-wrapping paper
crepe paper
contrasting paper for cut-out
   designs
ribbon

scissors
gummed tape
glue
pencil
tape measure

1. Cut the cardboard tubing to the length you want each snapper to be. Cut a piece of crepe paper large enough to cover the cardboard tube. Allow several inches of paper for each end of the snapper.

2. Using contrasting paper, cut out the design for decorating the outside of the snapper. Silhouettes of animals or snowflakes and lacy designs are very attractive.

3. For the inside of the snapper, you will first need a small surprise gift. It must be very tiny in order to leave room for two other items. Next, there should be a limerick or a poem, written especially for the person who will receive the snapper. And you should also include a paper hat (see page 46) folded as compactly as possible. The hat, poem, and gift are then placed inside the cardboard tube.

4. When the items are inside the tube, wrap the tube in the piece of crepe paper cut for that purpose. Then tie each end with a colorful ribbon. Glue the cut-out design you have made to the outside of the tube.

Advent Calendar

There are no strict rules for Advent calendar pictures. Half-timbered houses, villages, or forest scenes are often used, but the choice of picture is up to you.

Materials

2 pieces of smooth watercolor paper
watercolors
watercolor brush
heavy cardboard
scissors
pencil
ruler
X-acto knife
white glue
India ink and pen (optional)

1. When you have decided what scene you wish to have, cut one of the pieces of watercolor paper to the size you want your calendar to be, and draw your scene on it with pencil. Allow a ¼″ border for the edges of the design. This border will not be painted because there will be less danger of getting glue on the finished picture when the two paper pieces of the calendar are glued together.

front of Advent with numbered doors

"surprises" behind the Advent doors

66

2. Paint the scene you have drawn. When the paint is completely dry, choose the places where you want the doors to be. (Originally, the doors in Advent calendars dated from the 6th of December—the beginning of Advent—to the 24th. But today, most Advent calendars start on the 1st of December and end on the 24th.) Lightly outline each door with a pencil. With a pencil or pen and ink, mark each door with its appropriate number.

3. Place your picture on top of the cardboard and cut around three sides of each door with the X-acto knife.

4. When all the doors have been cut, place the second piece of watercolor paper (cut to the same size as the one on which the painting has been done) behind your painting. Make sure that all edges match evenly. Open the doors of the calendar and mark the spaces on the backing paper that show through the open doors. In these spaces on the backing sheet, draw the surprises to be found behind the doors of the finished calendar.

assembled Advent calendar with a few doors opened

5. Paint the little scenes, people, animals, or objects you have drawn on the backing sheet. When the paint is completely dry, neatly spread white glue ¼″ around the edges of the backing sheet. Place this sheet so that the paintings that will be behind the doors are properly aligned with the door openings.

Note: One thing to remember about a homemade, watercolor Advent calendar is that it must be guarded from sticky or wet hands. The least bit of water or dampness can ruin the design.

Straw Star-and-Wreath Mobile

Materials

rye straw (available in craft
   supply stores and florists)
red #10 crochet cotton

red thread
scissors
tape measure or ruler

1. Before you start constructing your mobile, you must prepare the straw. If you have purchased the straw in a craft supply shop, it will probably be husked and ready to soak. If you have cut your own straw or bought it in a florist shop, you must cut off the rye heads and cut out the nods that divide each straw into sections. Then you must remove the husks. Sort the straws according to size: thick, medium, and thin. Soak the straws in a pan or sink filled with water. If you use cold water, soak the straws overnight. If you soak the straws in very hot water, they should be ready within an hour or two. Because the straws must be submerged in water, they will have to be weighted down with a heavy object. The longer the straws are soaked, the yellower they will become. Soaking makes the straws more pliable and less prone to breakage when they are bent and tied into various shapes.

2. The top of the mobile—the piece from which all the other smaller pieces will be hung—will be in the shape of a large, six-pointed star. You will need twelve of the larger straws, each 7″ long, for this. The star is composed of two triangles; each side of these triangles consists of two straws. In pairs, tie six of the 7″ straws together with red crochet cotton to form an equilateral triangle, as shown in diagram 1. Make two of these triangles. Place one on top of the other to form a six-pointed star, as shown in diagram 2. Using the red crochet cotton, securely tie the triangles together at the points indicated in diagram 2. Cut three lengths of red thread, each 12″ long. Tie one thread to each of the three points, A, C, and E, according to diagram 2. Tie the top ends together so that the star will hang evenly. Carefully hang up the star so that the threads won't become tangled. When the smaller stars and wreaths have been completed, they will be suspended from this star.

3. Make the smaller stars by following the same instructions as for the larger stars, but use a single straw for each side instead of double straws. These straws should be thinner than those used for the large star. There should be six straws for each star. You should make nine

small stars of three different sizes: three 2″ stars; three 1½″ stars, and three 1″ stars. Cut eighteen 2″ straws, eighteen 1½″ straws, and eighteen 1″ straws. Assemble these the same way as the large star. First make two triangles, then join them together. Tie the small stars with thread instead of crochet cotton. The finished stars should resemble the one in diagram 3.

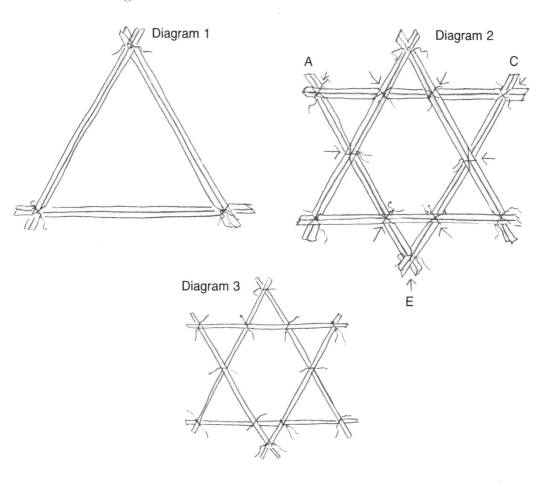

Diagram 1

Diagram 2

A

C

Diagram 3

E

4. You will need to make nine wreaths. Select eighteen medium straws, each 4″ long. Two straws will be used for each wreath. With the red thread, securely tie the ends of two straws together. Separate the two straws so that they form a right angle, as shown in diagram 4. Fold one straw, X, across the other, Y. Straw X is folded over Y from left to right; Y is folded from the bottom to the top, over X, as shown in diagram 5.

Then X is folded over Y from right to left, according to diagram 6. Y is folded over X from top to bottom, as shown in diagram 7. Repeat these steps with the rest of the 4″ straws. Then tie securely with thread, crossing over the two ends, as shown in diagram 8. Make all nine wreaths.

5. To assemble the mobile, cut twelve varying lengths of threads: six threads 7½″ long, three 6½″ long, and three 4″ long. To these, attach the stars and wreaths as follows:

To the six 7½″ threads, tie two of the 2″ stars, one 1½″ star, one 1″ star, and two wreaths.
To the three 6½″ threads, tie one 2″ star, one 1½″ star, and one wreath.
To the 4″ threads, tie the three remaining stars: one 1½″ star and two 1″ stars.

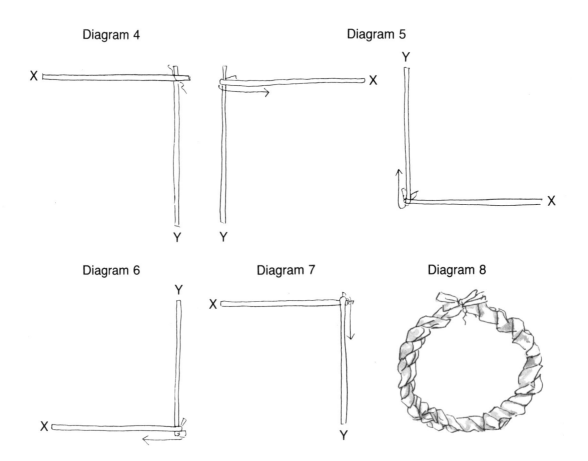

Diagram 4

Diagram 5

Diagram 6

Diagram 7

Diagram 8

Without cutting off the thread on the spool, tie the free end of it to point A of the star (at the crosspiece), as shown in diagram 9. Unroll more thread, but do not cut. Take the thread to the next point of the star and wrap it once around the crosspoint. Proceed to the next point and wrap the thread once around it. Continue doing this until the thread is back at the point at which you began, A. Cut the thread, leaving enough of it to tie to point A. There should now be a thread stretching between each point of the star. Tie each of the remaining wreaths to each thread, as shown in diagram 10.

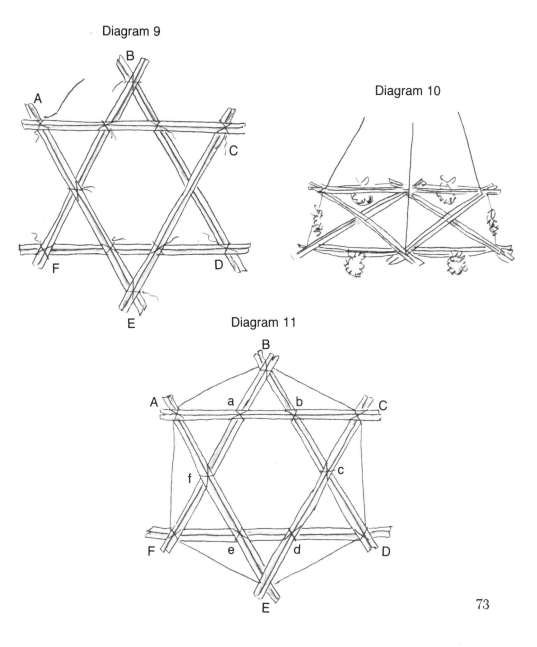

Diagram 9

Diagram 10

Diagram 11

6. The stars and wreaths will be suspended by their threads from points a, b, c, d, e, f, A, B, C, D, E, and F, as shown in diagram 11. Take the three stars with the 4″ threads and tie each to the star points a, c, and e. Take the two stars and one wreath with the 6½″ threads and tie each to points b, d, and f. Take the remaining four stars and two wreaths with the 7½″ threads and tie each to points A, B, C, D, E, and F. You can now hang up your mobile.

A straw star-and-wreath mobile should be hung in an area where there is slight air movement. Individual straw stars and wreaths make attractive year-round decorations; straw stars are often used as Christmas tree ornaments.

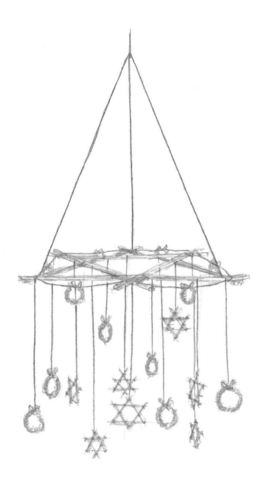

Paper-Lace Valentine and Envelope

This nostalgia valentine is made in the shape of a heart, but you can make one in any shape you wish. By following the basic directions, you can also create cards for other holidays and occasions.

There are two ways to make paper lace for valentines. One is to cut a folded piece of paper with a pair of scissors. The other method is to use an unfolded piece of paper and cut out the lace with an X-acto knife. Both of these methods will be used in making this valentine. A design for both the inside and outside of the card has been given, but once you know how to make the lace, you might like to create your own designs. Both scissors and knife must be *very sharp*. Dull tools will only lead to messy and torn work.

Materials

lightweight cardboard for templates
red construction paper
white drawing paper
heavy cardboard

finely pointed, sharp scissors
X-acto knife
white glue
pencil
ruler

Diagram 1

1. Cut templates out of the lightweight cardboard, following the two shapes shown in diagram 1. Cut one design out of red construction paper. This will be the body of the card. Following design B, cut two hearts out of the white drawing paper. These will be the lace decoration for the card. One of the hearts will be folded down the middle.

Diagram 2

2. Draw the design in diagram 2 on the heart that has been folded down the middle. Cut out the shaded area of the heart with the scissors. Then cut the lacework down the middle, as indicated in diagram 3. Carefully

Diagram 3

spread some white glue on the back side of the lacework and glue to the body of the valentine at the places indicated in diagram 4. These will form the cover of the valentine when it is completed.

Diagram 4

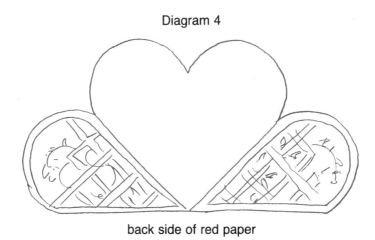

back side of red paper

3. Draw the design in diagram 5 on the heart which has not been folded in half. Lay the white heart on the piece of heavy cardboard with the design side facing up. Holding it carefully on top of the cardboard, cut out the shaded areas with the X-acto knife. This is done by pressing

Diagram 5

down firmly on the knife while drawing it around the lines you have penciled. Cutting lace in this way allows you to make a more complex design; the finished result will have a more "lacy" effect. However, it is also easier to tear the paper. Also, one must be very careful not to let the knife slip and slice a finger.

Diagram 6

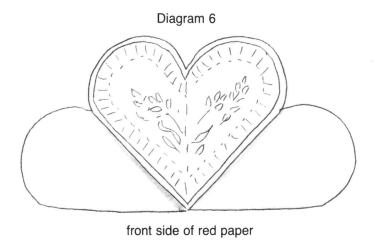

front side of red paper

4. When the lace has been cut, spread it with white glue and attach it to the space indicated in diagram 6. This is the inside of the card. Fold the card, as shown in diagram 7. The lace piece that was cut in half should meet in the middle to form the front. When parted, the cut-out lace design will be on the inside.

Diagram 7

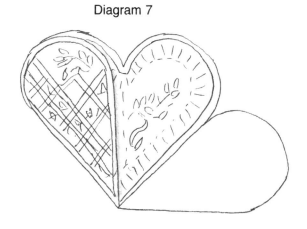

79

5. Making the envelope for this card is very simple to do. Cut two heart shapes from the white drawing paper. From the red construction paper, cut two strips measuring ¼″ × 3¼″ each and two strips measuring ¼″ × 1½″ each. Place the two white hearts together and glue on the strips, as indicated in diagram 8. These will hold the two hearts together. The card will fit neatly inside.

Diagram 8

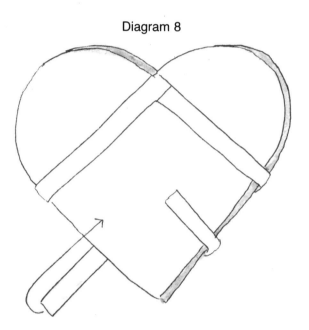

Valentine Mobile

A valentine mobile makes a charming substitute for a card, and is also a re-usable decoration for February 14th.

Materials

good quality, heavy, red con-
    struction paper
lightweight cardboard for tem-
    plates
white drawing paper
finely pointed, sharp scissors

drawing compass
needle
red thread
pencil
white glue

1. On a piece of the red construction paper, draw a circle 7½" in diameter with the compass. Following the design in diagram 1, cut a heart-shaped template out of the cardboard. At evenly spaced intervals around the inside of the circle, trace the heart six times, as shown in diagram 2. Cut out each of these heart shapes. The circle will form the top of the mobile, so it must be very carefully cut.

Diagram 1

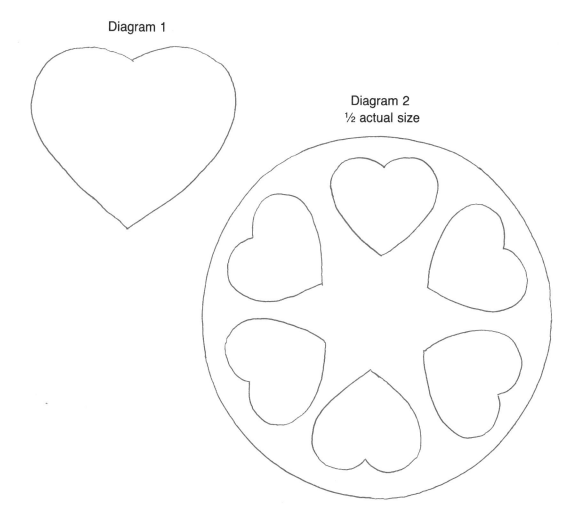

Diagram 2
½ actual size

2. Using the heart template, cut sixteen hearts out of the red construction paper. With the compass, draw a 1¼" circle in the center of each of the hearts. Cut out the circles, making sure you don't damage the hearts. These will hang from the large circle. Cut thirty-two ⅞" circles out of the red paper. With a compass, draw thirty-two ⅞" circles on the white drawing paper and cut them out. Fold each of these circles in half. In diagram 3, four cut-out designs are shown: a, b, c, and d. On eight of the circles, draw design A. On eight other circles, draw design b. On eight more circles, draw design c. On the remaining eight circles, draw design d. With a pair of sharply pointed scissors, cut out the shaded areas from the designs. (If the scissors you are using do not have very fine points and are not very sharp, you will find this step difficult.) Attach one design to each of the red ⅞" circles with white glue. While the glue is drying, cut the threads for hanging the hearts: one 13", three 10", six 8", and six 6½". Take one of the threads and glue it, at a point ⅜" down, to the undecorated side of one of the small circles. Take another one of the decorated circles and place its undecorated side to the undecorated side of the circle with the thread glued to it. Glue the circles together, sandwiching the thread between them. Repeat this step with all of the other threads and circles, matching the circles with a, b, c, and d designs.

Diagram 3

a	b	c	d

3. Take one of the heart-shaped pieces with a 1¼" circle cut out of it, and place a little glue at the top indentation on one side of the heart (see point g in diagram 4). Take one of the ⅞" decorated circles and center it within the 1¼" hole, so that the length of attached thread comes straight up along the indentation (point g) and through the glue. Repeat this step with each heart and decorated circle until all sixteen are assembled, as shown in diagram 5.

Diagram 4

G

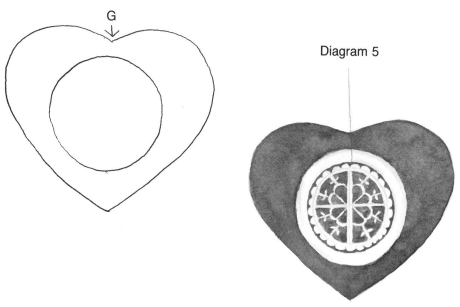

Diagram 5

Diagram 6

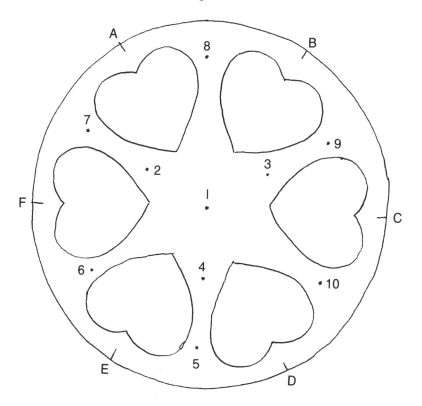

Diagram 7

4. Thread the needle with the 13″ length of thread attached to one of the hearts. Pass the needle up from underneath the large circle in the exact center, point 1. (The points are indicated in diagram 6.) Unthread the needle, leaving a 4″ end loose on top, and secure with a dab of glue at the needle hole. Let the glue dry completely before attaching the next heart. Repeat this step with the hearts with the 10″ threads, bringing them up through points 2, 3, and 4. Leave a 4½″ end at the top of each circle. Next, thread the hearts with the 8″ threads through points 5, 6, 7, 8, 9, and 10, leaving 5½″ ends. Make six ½″ slits around the outer edge of the circle at points A, B, C, D, E, and F, according to diagram 6. Take the hearts with the 6½″ threads and slip the threads into these slits, leaving a 5½″ end on top of the circle. Secure with a dab of glue. When all threads are in place and secured with glue, they should not slip through the needle holes or slits.

5. Gather together the ends of the threads at the top and tie them. There should be an even tension on each thread between the knot and the top of the circle where it is glued, as shown in diagram 7. At the knot, tie on an 8″ length of thread to hang up the mobile.

Cornucopia

The decorations for this cornucopia may be varied with painted trim or designs instead of cut-outs. The size may also be altered to suit a particular need. The finished cornucopia should be filled with a variety of nuts, candies, popcorn balls, and similar treats. Recipes for a number of these things are included in this book.

Materials

solid color or patterned wrapping paper
scissors
glue
stapler
pencil
ruler

1. Cut a 8½″ × 8½″ piece of the paper you have chosen. With the paper facing you so that it forms a diamond, bring the two side points of the diamond together and overlap them to form a tight cone, as shown in the diagram. Spread some glue along the overlapping edges to secure the cone.

2. Cut a straight piece of paper, about 18″ × 2½″, for the handle. This may be made of contrasting paper or the same paper used for the cornucopia. Fold this strip in thirds to form a handle, ¾″ × 18″ wide. Staple the handle to the opposite sides of the cone.

3. Cut a third piece of contrasting paper to fit around the top edge of the cone. Fold this in half, making sure that the design sides are on the inside. On the wrong side, draw the design you want to cut out for the trim. (We have given you one example of a design in the diagram.) There are infinite choices for trims—from simple fringes to ornate cutwork. Glue the trimming around the top edge of the cone.

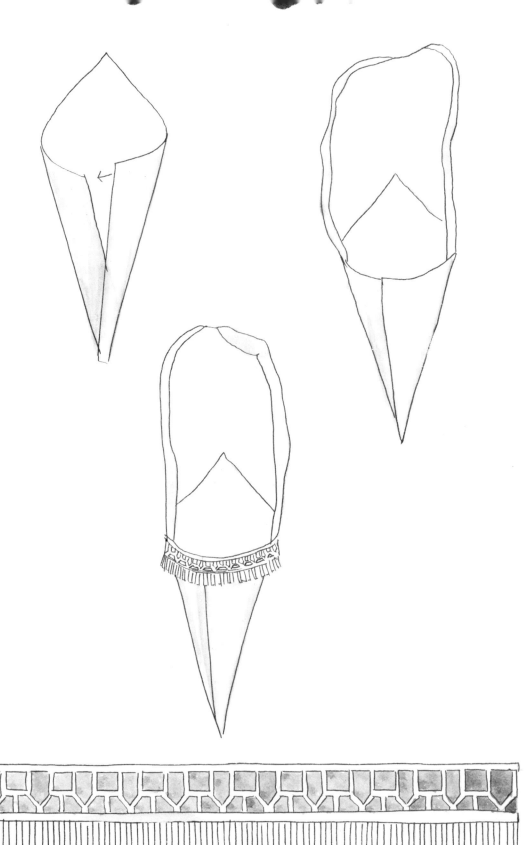

Cashew Butter Toffee

Ingredients
1 cup of sugar
½ teaspoon of salt
¼ cup of water
½ cup of butter
1 cup of chopped cashews
1 12-ounce package of semi-
   sweet chocolate chips

Materials
heavy saucepan
candy thermometer
greased cookie sheet
spatula
container and cover

1. Combine the sugar, salt, water, and butter in the saucepan. Over medium heat, cook the mixture to the "light-crack" (285° F.) stage. Add ½ cup of the chopped cashews and immediately pour the mixture onto the greased cookie sheet. Spread out and allow to cool.

2. Melt half of the chocolate chips and spread on the top of the cooled toffee. Sprinkle with half of the remaining chopped cashews. Let this mixture cool until the chocolate has hardened. Turn the mixture over and repeat the same process. Both sides of the toffee should be coated with chocolate and chopped nuts.

3. Break the toffee into pieces and store in a dry, covered container.

Thanksgiving Garden Relish

Ingredients
3 cups of chopped sweet green
    pepper
1 cup of chopped sweet red
    pepper
1 quart of chopped green
    tomato
1 cup of chopped onion
¼ cup of salt
1 quart of cider vinegar
¾ cup of sugar
1 tablespoon of mustard seed
½ tablespoon of celery seed

Materials
food chopper
saucepan
sterilized jars and seals

Chop all the vegetables with the coarse blade of a food chopper. Sprinkle them with the salt and let stand overnight. Drain. In a pan combine the vinegar, sugar, mustard seed, and celery seed. Bring them to the boiling point. Add the chopped vegetables and simmer for 10 minutes. Pour the mixture into hot, sterilized jars. Make certain that the vegetables are covered with the vinegar, then seal.
Yield: about 5 pints.

Fondant for Wintergreen or Peppermint Patties

Ingredients
3 tablespoons of light corn syrup
1 cup of water
3 cups of sugar

Materials
heavy-bottomed, 2-quart saucepan with cover
candy thermometer
marble slab, jelly-roll pan, or
   metal tray

pastry scraper, stout spatula, or
   painter's scraper (putty knife)
screw-top jar (3-cup capacity)
several layers of clean cheesecloth, each about 5″ × 5″

1. In a saucepan, dissolve the corn syrup with about ¼ cup of water. Pour in the rest of the water and the sugar. Over moderately high heat, swirl the pan gently, but do not stir the sugar syrup while the liquid is coming to a boil. Continue swirling until the liquid changes from cloudy to clear. Cover the pan, turn the heat on high, and boil the liquid for several minutes. Uncover, and insert the candy thermometer in the mixture. Continue boiling for a few more minutes, until the temperature reads 238° F—the softball stage.

2. Pour the syrup at once onto a marble slab or shallow pan. Let cool for about 10 minutes. When you press the fondant gently, and the surface wrinkles a bit, it is ready to knead.

3. With a scraper or spatula, knead the fondant vigorously until the syrup begins to whiten. This will take at least 5 minutes. Continue kneading until the syrup turns into a crumbly white mass, too stiff to be kneaded.

4. Ideally, the fondant should be allowed to "rest" overnight before using.
Yield: about 2 cups

Wintergreen Patties

Ingredients
fondant (see recipe, page 94)
2 tablespoons of light corn syrup
scant ¼ teaspoon of wintergreen
    oil
few drops of red food coloring

Materials
double boiler
candy thermometer
cookie sheet
waxed paper

1. Cut the fondant into small pieces and place them in a double boiler. Add the corn syrup, wintergreen oil, and food coloring. Over low heat, stir thoroughly while bringing the mixture to no more than 160° F. Do not bring the mixture to a heat lower than 150° F. because the finished patties will not harden.

2. With a teaspoon, drop the desired amounts of mixture onto a cookie sheet lined with waxed paper. In a few minutes, the patties will become firm and can be removed from the paper.

3. If the mixture becomes too hard when you are spooning it out, reheat it to 150–160° F. in the double boiler. If it is still too hard, add a few more drops of syrup while reheating the mixture.

4. Allow the patties to dry overnight before storing them in a dry, covered container. Place the fondant in the jar. Then dampen a few layers of cheesecloth and place the layers on top of the fondant. Tightly cover the jar and refrigerate.

Note: Peppermint patties can also be made by following the above recipe. Simply substitute peppermint oil for wintergreen oil and omit the red food coloring, or use green food coloring.

Satin Taffy

This taffy is not the chewy type. It acquires a creamy texture soon after it is finished.

Ingredients
3 cups of sugar
1 cup of boiling water
⅛ teaspoon of soda
½ teaspoon of salt
1 cup of cream
butter
essential oil of your choice (for
    flavoring)
cornstarch

Materials
heavy saucepan and cover
candy thermometer
buttered marble slab or cookie
    sheet
pastry scraper or heavy spatula
buttered kitchen shears
waxed paper

1. Combine the sugar, boiling water, soda, and salt in a saucepan. Stir over low heat until the mixture begins to boil and the sugar has dissolved. Cover the pan and continue to boil for about 3 minutes. Uncover the pan and cook, without stirring, until the candy thermometer reaches 236° F. Add the cream. Then cook, without stirring, until the syrup reaches 257° F. Pour the mixture at once onto a buttered marble slab or a cookie sheet. Do not scrape the pot.

2. Let the syrup cool slightly. Sprinkle the flavoring sparingly on the syrup. (Essential oils are very strong, and the taffy can be easily ruined if too much flavoring is used.) With a scraper or spatula, work the syrup until it is cool enough to handle. Lightly butter your hands and

carefully pick up the taffy. Remember that the candy will still be quite hot. Begin pulling the taffy between your two hands. Then fold it back, over itself. Stretch it out again and fold it back. Repeat this process until the taffy turns to a firm, glistening consistency. Then twist, pull, and fold the taffy until it becomes firm and opaque and has a satiny finish.

3. Form the taffy into a ball. Take a piece of the taffy and pull it away from the ball to form a rope about 1″ thick. Allow the rope to fall onto a surface you have previously dusted with cornstarch. Allow the taffy to cool. Then cut it into pieces with buttered shears, and wrap each piece in waxed paper.

Ruth's Chocolate Fudge

Ingredients
2 cups of sugar
2 squares of baker's chocolate or
   4 tablespoons of cocoa
½ cup of milk
1 tablespoon of butter
1 teaspoon of vanilla
½ cup of chopped nuts

Materials
heavy saucepan
candy thermometer
wooden spoon
buttered 8″ square baking pan

Combine the sugar, chocolate or cocoa, and milk in the saucepan. Bring the ingredients to a boil. *Do not stir,* or you will cause the mixture to become grainy. Bring the ingredients to the soft-ball stage (238° F.), then remove from the heat. Add the butter, vanilla, and chopped nuts. Beat the mixture vigorously with a wooden spoon until the fudge has cooled. Pour the fudge into the buttered baking pan and place it in the refrigerator to harden.

Note: For this fudge to turn out well, it is very important to remember two things. Do not stir the mixture when it has come to a boil. When the fudge reaches the soft-ball stage and you have added the remaining ingredients, beat the mixture continuously until cool, as previously mentioned. The longer you beat the fudge, the smoother it will be.

Linda's Butter-Jam Cookies

A tin filled with butter-jam cookies is a welcome gift, especially on Valentine's Day.

Ingredients

1 cup of butter
⅔ cup of sugar
1 egg
2½ cups of sifted flour
½ teaspoon of salt

1 teaspoon of vanilla
jam (raspberry, apricot, or
    pineapple)
powdered sugar

Materials

mixing bowl and utensils
waxed paper
plastic bag
rolling pin
¾″ round, fluted-edged cookie
    cutter

small heart-shaped canapé cut-
    ter
ungreased cookie sheet
sifter

1. Preheat the oven to 350° F. Cream together the butter and sugar until light and soft. Add the egg and beat it with the butter-sugar mixture. Add the sifted flour, salt, and vanilla. Mix the ingredients thoroughly and form into a ball. Wrap the dough in waxed paper and place it in a plastic bag. Seal the bag and refrigerate the dough for several hours.

2. Roll out the dough and cut out an even number of cookies with the cookie cutter. For each completed cookie you will need to cut out two rounds. Use the small canapé cutter to cut a heart shape out of the middle of half of the rounds. These halves, with the heart-shaped holes in the center, will be the tops of the cookies.

3. Place the cookies without the holes on the cookie sheet, and put a small spoonful of jam on them. Top each of the halves with a cookie with a hole, and seal them around the edges. Bake until golden brown. Remove to a cooling rack. When the cookies have thoroughly cooled, use a sifter to sprinkle the tops with powdered sugar. Dab a little more jam on the heart cut-outs. Store the cookies in a dry, covered tin.

T. Tudor

Popcorn Balls

The following recipe makes about 15 balls. When they are cooled, wrap each ball in clear cellophane or plastic wrap and tie the tops with colorful ribbons. These balls fit nicely in the tops of cornucopias (see page 87).

Ingredients
¼ cup of butter
1 cup of brown sugar
½ cup of light corn syrup
⅔ cup of sweetened condensed
    milk
½ teaspoon of vanilla
5 quarts of popped corn
butter

Materials
heavy saucepan
large spoon
candy thermometer

Combine the butter, sugar, and corn syrup in the saucepan. Stir well and bring to a boil over medium heat. Add the condensed milk and stir. Simmer the mixture, while stirring constantly, until it reaches the soft-ball stage (238° F.). Add the vanilla and stir. Pour the mixture over the popped corn, making sure that all pieces are coated. Lightly butter your hands and shape the popcorn into balls of about 3″ in diameter.

Almond Brittle

Ingredients
1 cup of blanched almonds
½ cup of sugar
3 tablespoons of water

Materials
roasting pan or cookie sheet
small, heavy saucepan and cover
lightly oiled cookie sheet

1. Preheat the oven to 350° F. Spread the almonds on a cookie sheet or in a roasting pan, and set the pan in the middle of the oven. Toast the almonds for about 10 to 15 minutes, stirring them several times during the toasting. When they are lightly browned, remove them from the oven.

2. Combine the sugar and water in the saucepan and set it over high heat. Swirl the mixture in the pan but do not stir while it is coming to a boil. When the syrup changes from cloudy to clear, cover and allow the mixture to boil for several minutes, or until the syrup's bubbles become thick. Remove the cover and continue boiling, until the syrup turns a light caramel brown. Remove from the heat and stir in the toasted almonds at once.

3. Pour the mixture onto the oiled cookie sheet and allow it to harden. This will take about 15 minutes. Break the brittle into pieces.
Yield: about 1 cup

Hot Cross Buns

Ingredients
2 cups of flour
½ cup of sugar
powdered sugar (for frosting)
1 cake of yeast
1 cup of warm milk
cold milk (for frosting)
½ cup of melted butter
1 cup of currants
¼ teaspoon of salt
½ teaspoon of cinnamon

Materials
bowl
greased cookie sheets

1. Mix together the flour, sugar, cinnamon, and currants. Dissolve the yeast in the warm milk and add to the dry ingredients. Let the mixture rise for about 30 minutes.

2. Add the salt and warm (not hot) melted butter to the dough. Let the dough rise for 30 minutes.

3. Preheat the oven to 350°. Shape the dough into buns and place them on greased cookie sheets. Let the buns rise. Bake until delicately browned. Yield: approximately 12 buns.

4. For the crosses on the buns, mix powdered sugar with a little cold milk until the mixture is thick enough to hold its shape.

Halloween Candied Apples

Ingredients
1 cup of sugar
⅔ cup of water
pinch of cream of tartar
a few drops of red food coloring
butter

Materials
heavy saucepan and cover
large shallow pan, filled with
    hot water
skewers or popsicle sticks
buttered cookie sheet

1. Bring the sugar, water, and cream of tartar to a boil. Continue boiling, covered, for several minutes, or until the syrup reaches 300° F.

2. Remove from the heat and add a few drops of red food coloring. Place the pan with the syrup mixture over hot water.

3. Stick skewers or popsicle sticks into the apples, and dip the fruit into the syrup, making sure that each apple is covered with the mixture. Place the apples on a well-buttered cookie sheet to harden.

Rye Bread

Ingredients

2 cakes or 2 packages of yeast

4 tablespoons of melted shortening

1 teaspoon of sugar

1 cup of brown sugar

1 quart of lukewarm water

4 tablespoons of molasses

1 tablespoon of salt

3 cups of rye flour

white flour (see instructions)

pinch of baking soda

Materials

saucepans

greased bowl

3 bread pans, each 8½ × 4½ × 2⅝",
or a large cookie sheet

1. Add the sugar to the lukewarm water and dissolve the yeast in the mixture. Add enough white flour to make a soft, sponge-like mixture. Let the sponge stand in a warm place until it becomes bubbly.

2. Heat the molasses and add the baking soda and melted shortening. Add this mixture to the sponge. Then add the brown sugar, salt, and rye flour. Beat vigorously.

3. Add enough white flour to the dough to make it stiff enough to knead. Knead the dough for about 10 minutes, then place it in a greased bowl. Cover the bowl with a towel, and allow the dough to rise in a warm place until it has doubled in bulk. Knead, and let rise again. Shape the dough into three loaves and allow them to rise.

4. Preheat the oven to 350°. The loaves may be baked in bread pans or they may be shaped into three round loaves and baked on a cookie sheet. Baking time: approximately 45 minutes.

Note: Because this bread freezes well, you might like to wrap the loaves in heavy aluminum foil for the recipient's freezer.

New England Cranberry Sauce

Ingredients
2 pounds of cranberries (fresh,
    not frozen)
enough water to barely cover
    the berries when pressed
    down
2 pounds of sugar

Materials
heavy saucepan
wooden spoon
1 quart jelly mold

1. Add the water and sugar to cranberries. Bring to a simmer and skim occasionally. Continue cooking until the juice jells when dropped on a cold plate.

2. Pour the mixture into a jelly mold. Allow the sauce to harden. When ready to serve, unmold onto a plate. If you plan to give both the sauce and the mold as a gift, first cover the mold in two layers of plastic wrap.

Toffee Bar Cookies

Ingredients
1 cup of butter
1 cup of light brown sugar
1 egg yolk
2 cups of sifted flour
12-ounce package of chocolate
    chips
chopped nuts

Materials
bowl
greased cookie sheet
icing spreader

1. Preheat the oven to 350°. Cream together the butter and sugar. Add the egg yolk and sifted flour. Mix thoroughly. Spread the dough on a greased cookie sheet and bake for fifteen minutes.

2. Remove the dough from the oven and sprinkle it with the chocolate chips. Return it to the oven for a minute or two, or until the chocolate chips have melted. Take the baked cookie sheet out of the oven and spread the melted chocolate over it. Sprinkle with chopped nuts. Cut the sheet into squares while it is still warm.

Raisin Gingerbread Cakes

Ingredients
½ cup of sugar or 6–7 table-
    spoons of honey
½ cup of butter
1 beaten egg
1 cup of molasses
2½ cups of flour
1½ teaspoons of soda
1 teaspoon of cinnamon
1 teaspoon of ginger
½ teaspoon of ground cloves
½ teaspoon of salt
1 cup of hot water
1 cup of raisins

Materials
2 bowls
greased muffin tins

1. Cream the butter and the sugar or honey until light. Add the beaten egg and molasses. Sift the flour with the soda, cinnamon, ginger, clove, and salt. Add the raisins to the dry ingredients, then add the hot water and the first four ingredients. Beat until the mixture is smooth.

2. Preheat the oven to 350°. Fill the muffin tins with the gingerbread batter and bake for approximately 25 minutes.

Note: We prefer to bake our gingerbread cakes in iron muffin tins, but aluminum tins may be substituted.

Common Metric Equivalents
and Conversions

Approximate

1 inch	=	25 millimeters
1 foot	=	0.3 meter
1 yard	=	0.9 meter
1 square inch	=	6.5 square centimeters
1 square foot	=	0.09 square meter
1 square yard	=	0.8 square meter
1 millimeter	=	0.04 inch
1 meter	=	3.3 feet
1 meter	=	1.1 yards
1 square centimeter	=	0.16 square inch

Accurate to Parts Per Million

inches × 25.4	=	millimeters
feet × 0.3048	=	meters
yards × 0.9144	=	meters
square inches × 6.4516	=	square centimeters
square feet × 0.092903	=	square meters
square yards × 0.836127	=	square meters

Temperature Conversion

The Celsius scale (C), often called the centigrade scale, is derived from the Fahrenheit scale by the following formula:

$$C = \frac{5(F-32)}{9}$$